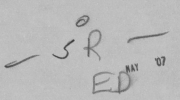

MAKE it WORK!

OCEANS

Andrew Haslam & Barbara Taylor

Consultant: Rachel Mills BSc, PhD
Southampton Oceanography Centre

World Book

World Book, Inc.
233 N. Michigan Avenue
Suite 2000
Chicago, IL 60601
in association with Two-Can Publishing.

Text: Barbara Taylor
Editor: Jacqueline McCann
Managing Editor: Christine Morley
Art Director: Carole Orbell
Senior Designer: Gareth Dobson
Production: Leila Peerun
Photography: John Englefield
Model-makers: Peter Griffiths, Melanie Williams

2004 revised printing
© Two-Can Publishing, 1997
Series concept and original design © Andrew Haslam

**For information about other World Book publications, visit our Web site
http://www.worldbook.com or call 1-800-WORLDBK (967-5325). For information
about sales to schools and libraries call 1-800-975-3250 (United States);
1-800-837-5365 (Canada).**

The Library of Congress has cataloged a previous edition of this title as follows:

Library of Congress Cataloging-in-Publication Data

Haslam, Andrew.
   Oceans / Andrew Haslam & Barbara Taylor.
     p. cm – (Make-it-work! Geography)
   Includes index.
   Summary: Explains the characteristics of oceans and the forces and principles which
act upon them, demonstrating with experiments and models.
   ISBN 0-7166-5110-6 (hc) – ISBN 0-7166-5111-4 (sc)
     1. Oceans–Juvenile literature. [1. Oceanography–Experiments.
2. Experiments.] I. Taylor, Barbara, 1954-. II. Title. III. Series.
GC21.5.H37 1997
551.46 dc21   97-3316

ISBN (this edition) 0-7166-5123-8

Photographic credits:
Britstock-Ifa/Bernd Ducke p7; Bruce C. Heezen and Marie Tharp © Marie Tharp 1977 p5;
Dr Ken Macdonald/Science Photo Library p11; Mark Edwards/Still Pictures p37;
Oxford Cartographers (map) p43; Planet Earth Pictures/Gary Bell p28; Planet Earth Pictures/John Bracegirdle p21;
Planet Earth Pictures/John Eastcott/Yva Momatiuk p26; Planet Earth Pictures/Robert Hessler p30;
Rex Features/Rob Howarth p25; Simon Fraser/Science Photo Library p45; Tony Stone p18;
Tony Stone/Randy Wells p4; Tony Stone/Ted Wood p38; Zefa/M. Hoshino p14.

Printed in China

5 6 7 8 9 10 09 08 07 06 05 04

Contents

Studying oceans

Geography helps us to understand what happened to the Earth in the past, how it is changing now, and what might happen to it in the future. Understanding oceans is an important part of geography because oceans cover over 70 percent of the Earth's surface. People who study oceans are called **oceanographers**. They try to understand how seawater moves around the world, how the oceans were formed, and what effects oceans have on coastlines.

Exploring oceans
Studying the oceans is rather like studying outer space. Both places are remote and mysterious, and scientists need special equipment to survive there and to carry out experiments. The deepest parts of the Earth's surface lie beneath the oceans. We have only recently begun to explore these hidden places.

◁ *Oceanographers use information from **satellites** and **sonar** to learn more about the ocean.*

△ *Over millions of years, the Pacific Ocean has pounded the east coast of Australia and created these cliffs.*

Life in the oceans
Life on Earth probably evolved in the oceans about 3½ million years ago. Today, an amazing variety of creatures lives in the sea, from the largest animal that ever lived, the blue whale, to microscopic organisms called **plankton**. The deepest parts of the ocean are more than 36,000 feet (11,000 m) below sea level, so it is difficult to study them. Oceanographers are still finding new forms of life in the oceans. Recently, they discovered giant tubeworms around underwater volcanoes.

Oceans and people
Almost everyone depends on oceans to some degree. Oceans have an important effect on the world's weather. They are also an important source of food, and people use them for travel, trade, and sports. We also take oil and minerals from beneath the seabed and use the energy of the tides to create power. The way that we treat the oceans today will affect the Earth, the oceans, and the creatures that live in them in the future.

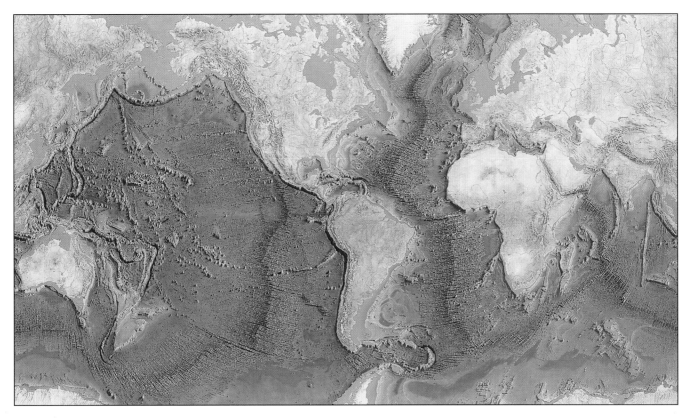

△ *There are mountain ranges under the sea, as well as on land. The long ridges running between the continents are mountain ranges many thousands of miles long.*

Oceanography today

Studying the oceans brings together different subjects. Some oceanographers study the land at the edge of oceans and the rocks under the seabed. This area of study is called **geology**. Others concentrate on seawater itself—how hot or cold it is, how much salt it contains, and how **ocean currents** move around the globe. Marine biologists study sea creatures and try to understand how they interact with their environment.

Throughout this book, we have used symbols to show where information relates to particular topics. The symbols are:

geology	🏔	tides, waves, currents	𝍌
temperature	🌡	seawater	≋
marine life	🐟	energy	⛏
human	👫	mapmaking	✎

Make it Work!

The Make it Work! way of looking at geography is to carry out experiments that will help you understand how geography shapes the world we live in. By studying the models, you will discover more about the oceans.

▽ *Some experiments in this book will help you understand how water in the oceans moves around the world.*

The world's oceans

There are three main oceans on Earth: the Pacific, Atlantic, and Indian. There are also two smaller ones: the Arctic and the Southern, or Antarctic. They flow into each other, so you could say that there is really only one vast ocean. Each ocean contains smaller areas of water called seas, bays, or gulfs, which are all partly enclosed by land.

♦ Temperature of the oceans

The temperature in the oceans and seas varies from one place to another and from the surface to the ocean floor. The waters of the Arctic and Southern oceans are icy cold. However, tropical seas, such as the Caribbean, are much warmer. All the water in the oceans constantly flows around the Earth. Cold water, which is heavier than warm water, sinks at the North and South poles, then flows along the ocean floor toward the equator. At the equator, the water becomes warmer and rises. Then it flows back to the poles.

▷ *Viewed from this side, the Earth seems to be all water. The Pacific Ocean covers one-third of the globe.*

The Mariana Trench lies 35,840 feet (10,924 m) below sea level.

The Ring of Fire in the Pacific is where lots of volcanoes erupt and earthquakes happen.

Thousands of volcanic and coral islands are dotted around the Pacific.

The Great Barrier Reef lies off the coast of Australia.

The Arctic Ocean is almost completely surrounded by land.

The Hawaiian Islands are part of a chain of underwater volcanoes.

In the Caribbean Sea, there are many coral reefs.

The Southern Ocean is also known as the Antarctic Ocean.

Arctic Ocean

Asia

North America

Pacific Ocean

South America

Oceania

Southern Ocean

Antarctica

The Pacific Ocean

This is the largest ocean in the world. It is also the deepest, with an average depth of 12,900 feet (3,940 m). There are many deep valleys, or **ocean trenches**, around the edge of the Pacific, along the east coast of Asia and the west coast of South America. The Mariana Trench, off the coast of the Philippines, is the deepest place on Earth.

The Southern Ocean

This ocean is located around the continent of Antarctica. The waters of the Pacific, Atlantic, and Indian oceans all mingle in the Southern Ocean, just above Antarctica. More than half of the Southern Ocean freezes over in winter. In summer, some of the ice melts, breaks up, and drifts out to nearby oceans as pack ice.

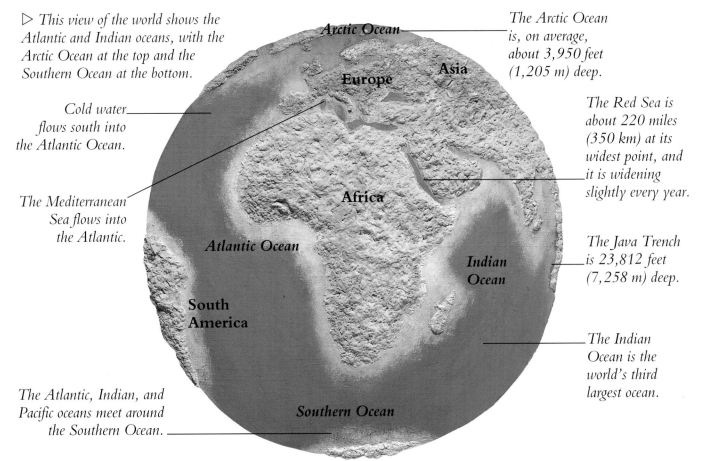

◁ *Two percent of all the water in the Arctic Ocean is frozen in huge icebergs like this.*

The Arctic Ocean

The Arctic is the world's smallest and shallowest ocean. It is unusual compared to other oceans because it is almost completely surrounded by land—Asia, North America, Greenland, and Europe. It is also covered by a thick layer of ice for six months of the year. Beneath every ocean are huge dips in the Earth's crust called **ocean basins**. The Arctic Ocean has four basins.

▷ *This view of the world shows the Atlantic and Indian oceans, with the Arctic Ocean at the top and the Southern Ocean at the bottom.*

Cold water flows south into the Atlantic Ocean.

The Mediterranean Sea flows into the Atlantic.

The Atlantic, Indian, and Pacific oceans meet around the Southern Ocean.

Arctic Ocean

Europe

Asia

Africa

Atlantic Ocean

Indian Ocean

South America

Southern Ocean

The Arctic Ocean is, on average, about 3,950 feet (1,205 m) deep.

The Red Sea is about 220 miles (350 km) at its widest point, and it is widening slightly every year.

The Java Trench is 23,812 feet (7,258 m) deep.

The Indian Ocean is the world's third largest ocean.

The Atlantic Ocean

This is the world's second largest ocean. It covers about one-fifth of the Earth's surface. The Atlantic has the greatest number of shallow seas. These include the Gulf of Mexico, the Caribbean Sea, and the Mediterranean Sea. The Atlantic is also less salty than other oceans because a lot of fresh water flows into it from rivers on the surrounding continents.

The Indian Ocean

Along the floor of the ocean runs a long chain of underwater volcanic mountains called a **mid-ocean ridge**. The ridge in the Indian Ocean connects with those in the Pacific and the Atlantic (see picture page 5). The deepest point in the Indian Ocean is the Java Trench. There are also many **coral reefs**, including the Maldive and Seychelle islands, dotted around this ocean.

Birth of an ocean

When the Earth formed some 4½ billion years ago, there were no oceans. Most scientists say that rain collected in dips on the Earth's surface to make oceans. Over millions of years, the shape of the land and the ocean basins has changed. They are still changing because heat from inside the Earth makes the outer crust move.

⛰ Rocks on the move

The Earth is made up of three main layers: the crust, the **mantle**, and the core. The crust is the outermost layer of the Earth. The mantle is made up of hot rocks. As the rocks melt and combine with gases, they form **magma** and rise up near the crust. When magma erupts through cracks in the crust, either on land or underwater, it creates volcanoes. When it cools, it turns into solid rock. Where magma rises through a mid-ocean ridge, it makes new ocean floor.

⛰ How the oceans formed

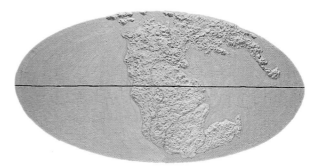

1 About 250 million years ago, there was one main land mass surrounded by one vast ocean.

⛰ Ridges and trenches

As magma erupts through the ocean floor, it is forced upward, forming mountain ranges, long mid-ocean ridges. Over millions of years, the old ocean floor is pushed slowly outward, away from the ridge. When part of the ocean floor is pushed into the edge of another, one edge gets forced down under the other, sometimes creating a deep trench.

▽ *This model shows how hot rocks in the Earth's mantle force their way through the crust, creating new ocean floor.*

Magma rises through a mid-ocean ridge, cools, and makes new seabed.

underwater volcano

Earth's crust

New ocean floor pushes old ocean floor slowly over millions of years.

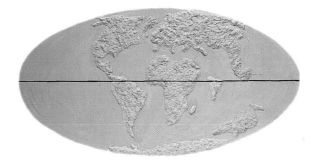

2 By 200 million years ago, the land had begun to separate and water filled in the spaces.

3 By about 60 million years ago, the positions of the land and oceans were similar to those of today.

volcanoes erupting on land

a continent

Magma also rises underneath the continents.

An ocean trench forms where ocean floor is forced under the edge of another piece of land.

Moving continents

The Earth's crust is broken up into about 30 pieces, like the cracked shell of a hard-boiled egg. These pieces are called plates. The plates drift on top of the Earth's mantle, moving a few centimeters a year. Over millions of years, these small movements can tear continents apart, leaving huge ocean basins. Where the **Earth's plates** meet, mid-ocean ridges and trenches form.

Plate movement

Plates may move apart, move together, or slide past each other. At ocean ridges, plates move apart, whereas at trenches they push together. Often, volcanoes erupt and earthquakes happen along the edges of plates, where the Earth's crust is unstable, or weak.

MAGMA EXPERIMENT

Ask an adult to help you.

You will need: bowl, cooking oil, red food coloring, sterno candle, stand, matches, eyedropper

1 Pour the oil into the bowl. Place the bowl on the stand, with the candle underneath. Now light the candle and warm the oil.

2 Using the eyedropper, squeeze a few drops of food coloring onto the bottom of the bowl, above the flame.

Result: The food coloring warms and rises. When it reaches the surface, it spreads out, cools, and sinks back down. This is similar to how magma behaves.

The ocean floor

The landscape under the oceans is even more varied than on dry land. Mountain ranges are longer, valleys are wider and deeper, and slopes are steeper. One reason for this is that rivers wash enormous amounts of **sediment** into the sea. Another is that magma constantly erupts along mid-ocean ridges, forming new ocean floor.

The continental shelf
From the edges of the continents, the land slopes gently downward. The sea is not very deep here, perhaps only about 430 feet (130 m) deep. This shallow ledge of ocean floor is called the **continental shelf**.

The continental slope and rise
At the edge of the continental shelf, a steep slope drops about 2¼ miles (3.6 km) to the ocean floor. This is the continental slope. In many places, sediment is washed down to the bottom of the slope, forming a ridge called a continental rise.

The deep-ocean floor
Between 14,000 and 18,000 feet (4,300 and 5,500 m) below the surface of the sea are vast, flat areas of ocean floor called **abyssal plains**. These plains are covered in thick layers of sediment. In some places, deep-ocean currents flowing across abyssal plains form large mud waves in the sediment.

▽ *If you could drain all the water out of an ocean, you would see some of these features. This model shows a section of ocean floor thousands of miles across.*

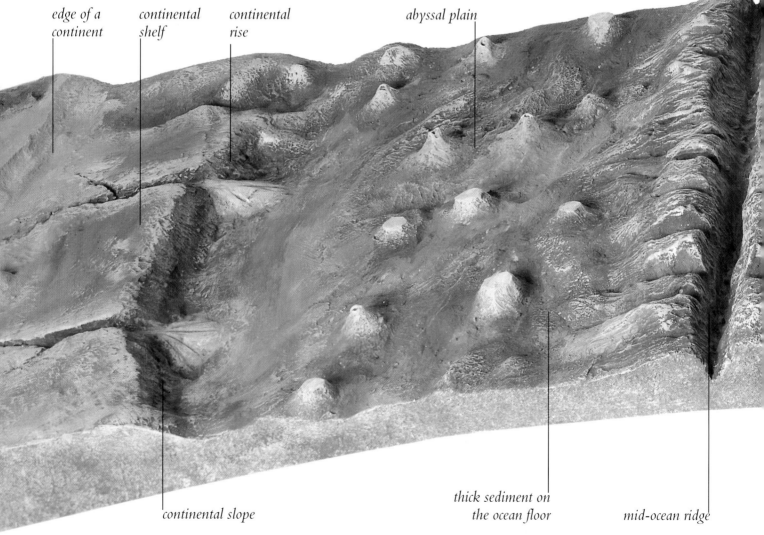

edge of a continent

continental shelf

continental rise

abyssal plain

continental slope

thick sediment on the ocean floor

mid-ocean ridge

◁ *This image was made using sonar signals (see pages 42 and 43). It shows part of the mid-ocean ridge in the Pacific. The deepest parts are dark blue, and the shallowest are pink.*

🏔 Seamounts

Sometimes, magma forces its way through an abyssal plain. When this happens, underwater volcanic mountains called **seamounts** form. Some seamounts are flat-topped. These are called **guyots**. Their tops are probably worn away by waves over thousands of years. Most seamounts are found in groups or chains. When they rise above the sea surface, seamounts become islands. The Hawaiian Islands are a chain of seamounts.

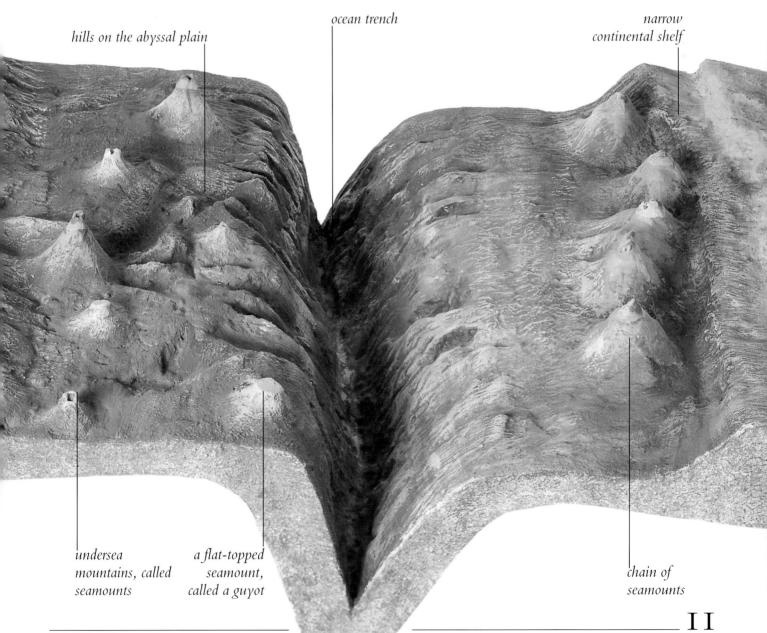

hills on the abyssal plain

ocean trench

narrow continental shelf

undersea mountains, called seamounts

a flat-topped seamount, called a guyot

chain of seamounts

Seawater

Seawater undergoes many changes from the surface to the ocean floor. Surface water is warm because it is penetrated by sunlight, whereas water near the seabed is cold and dark. The weight of all the water pressing down on the seabed also means that the pressure is much greater there. Seawater contains dissolved minerals and salt, but the amounts vary from ocean to ocean.

▷ *This model shows the depth to which people can dive using special equipment.*

≋ ♔ Water pressure

As you go deeper under the sea, more water presses down on you. At the surface there is hardly any pressure. But people cannot dive to the bottom of the ocean because the pressure would crush them as easily as you can crush an egg on land. Instead, people descend in small submarines called **submersibles**. These vehicles are made to withstand the enormous pressure of the watery depths.

≋ Why is the sea blue?

Although water is colorless, the sea often appears blue-green. This is because blue and green light (two of the colors you see in a rainbow) reach deeper below the surface than the other colors. Tiny particles in water also scatter blue and green light, spreading it through the water. The sea also reflects the color of the sky, making it seem blue or gray, depending on the weather.

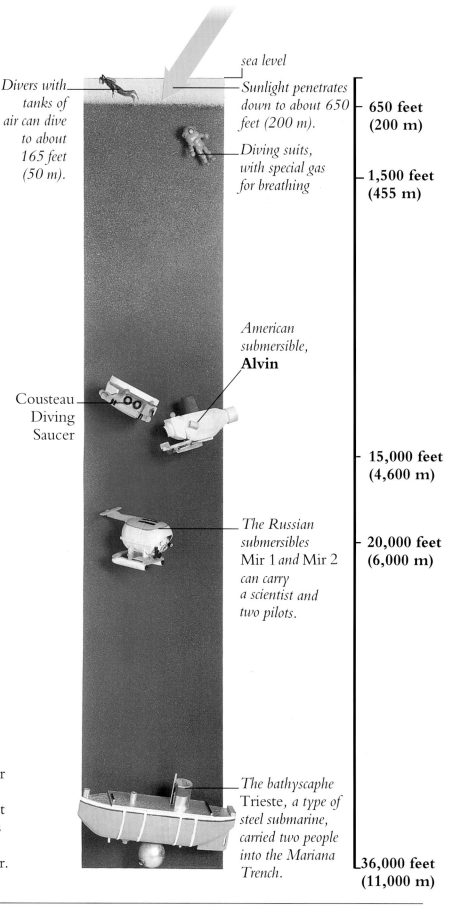

Divers with tanks of air can dive to about 165 feet (50 m).

sea level

Sunlight penetrates down to about 650 feet (200 m).

Diving suits, with special gas for breathing

American submersible, **Alvin**

Cousteau Diving Saucer

The Russian submersibles Mir 1 *and* Mir 2 *can carry a scientist and two pilots.*

The bathyscaphe Trieste, *a type of steel submarine, carried two people into the Mariana Trench.*

650 feet (200 m)

1,500 feet (455 m)

15,000 feet (4,600 m)

20,000 feet (6,000 m)

36,000 feet (11,000 m)

WATER PRESSURE TEST

You will need: long plastic tube, balloon, tank or bucket of water

1 Attach the balloon to the tube.

2 Blow up the balloon. You should find that the balloon is easy to blow up.

3 Now place the balloon in the tank, near the surface of the water. Blow up your balloon again.

Result: It should be more difficult than in step 2 because of the pressure of the water pressing on the balloon.

4 Place the balloon at the bottom of the tank and blow up the balloon again.

Result: It will be a lot more difficult this time, because the pressure at the bottom of the tank is greater than at the surface.

🌡 Water temperature

The temperature of the surface of an ocean varies from one part to another. In warm, shallow waters, it may reach 86 °F (30 °C). In the cold polar oceans, temperatures drop to 28 °F (-2 °C). Surface temperatures also change with the seasons, but the temperature at the ocean floor tends to stay the same all year, at about 34 to 39 °F (1 to 4 °C).

〰 Why is the sea salty?

Some of the salts and minerals in seawater are washed off the land by rivers. Other salts come from gases released by volcanoes on land. The gases mix with rain, which falls on the sea. Still more salts escape from cracks in the ocean floor.

〰 Why does seawater rise and fall?

All these salts and minerals in seawater make it dense. Density means how heavy something is for its size. Water that is dense and cold, sinks. Water that is less dense and warm, rises. This means that the density of seawater affects the way water moves through the oceans (see pages 16 and 17). To measure water density, we use a hydrometer.

MAKE A HYDROMETER

You will need: glass, straw, modeling clay, tape, water, salt

1 Attach a blob of clay to one end of the straw. Your straw is a hydrometer, and with it you will be able to test the density of water.

salt water

fresh water

2 Place the straw in a glass of water that is room temperature. With tape, mark the straw where it meets the surface of the water. Now add salt to the water.

Result: The straw floats higher because salt water is denser than fresh water. The salt in the water pushes up against the straw and helps hold it nearer the surface.

Frozen oceans

During winter, huge areas of the Arctic and Southern oceans freeze. In the Southern Ocean, the ice spreads out across the sea from the edge of the ice-covered continent of Antarctica. In the Arctic, however, there is no land, only a thick sheet of ice on top of the ocean. In summer, half of the ice melts, and the waters warm up slightly. Then, the Arctic becomes a rich feeding ground for whales and other wildlife.

△ *In the summer, humpback whales migrate to the Arctic Ocean to feed in the plankton-rich waters.*

Why the Arctic Ocean is frozen

For six months of the year, the Arctic Ocean is plunged into freezing darkness. This is because the North Pole is tilted away from the sun. The waters of the Arctic receive less heat than waters at, or near, the equator because they are not heated directly by the sun. The dazzling ice sheet also reflects back 95 percent of the heat from the sun, which helps keep temperatures extremely cold.

▷ *This model shows winter in the Arctic Ocean, when sea ice covers an area one-and-a-half times the size of Canada.*

Icebergs

Icebergs are large chunks of ice that break off the ends of **glaciers** at the edge of the sea. The biggest ones, which are found in the Southern Ocean, tower up to 400 feet (120 m) above the water and are many miles long. Icebergs float because when water freezes, it takes up more space, which makes it lighter, or less dense, than water.

Long slicks of ice are called grease ice.

Pancake ice is freezing slush broken up by winds and waves into round pieces.

Pancake and grease ice join to form ice floes, which move with the winds and currents.

Icebreakers force their way through an ice floe.

♪ When seawater freezes

Fresh water freezes at 32 °F (0 °C), but seawater freezes at a slightly lower temperature. It is the salts in the water that make seawater freeze at a lower temperature.

♫ ♪ Sinking seawater

When ice forms, most of the salt in the water is left behind in the sea, so icebergs are made of fresh water. This means that the surface of the sea underneath an iceberg is saltier than usual. The extra-salty water is denser than normal seawater, so it sinks. Sinking cold water helps to push water around the world's oceans and is an important driving force behind the world's ocean currents.

FLOATING ICEBERG TEST

You will need: water, plastic bag, tank or sink

1 Pour some water into the plastic bag. Tie the bag tightly and place it in a freezer overnight.

2 Remove the iceberg from the bag and float it in a tank of water.

Result: Although 85 to 90 percent of the iceberg will lie below the water level, the iceberg will still float. This is because ice is less dense than water.

Most Arctic icebergs break off the ends of glaciers in Greenland.

Whales migrate south at the start of the Arctic winter.

Small icebergs, called bergy bits, are about the size of an average house.

Only 10 to 15 percent of an iceberg is above water.

Icebergs are eventually carried into the Atlantic Ocean by ocean currents.

Ocean currents

Ocean currents are "rivers" of water that flow on, or near, the surface of the ocean or deep underwater. They are caused by the wind, the spin of the Earth, and differences in the density of water. Ocean currents may be warm or cold, depending on where they have come from.

℟ Surface currents

Currents in the top 1,500 feet (455 m) of the ocean are called surface currents. They travel about 6 miles (10 km) a day and are driven mainly by the wind. Because of the Earth's spin, the world's winds and surface currents veer sideways. This is called the **Coriolis effect**. The winds, along with the shapes of the continents, make surface currents flow in five large loops, called **gyres**. The gyres south of the equator flow into each other above Antarctica because there is no land to stop them.

▽ *This map shows warm surface currents in red and cold ones in blue. The thickest lines show the strongest currents.*

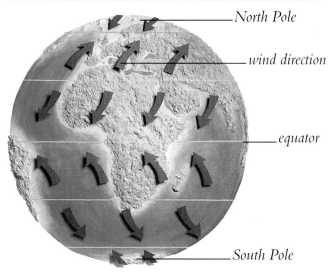

North Pole

wind direction

equator

South Pole

△ *The world's winds blow in six main bands, pulling the surface of the oceans along with them.*

℟ ⚓ Currents and climate

The equator receives more of the sun's heat than the poles. Ocean currents and winds help spread this heat around the Earth. Warm surface currents flow away from the equator toward the poles, carrying heat with them. This circulation of heat prevents places near the equator from becoming hotter and hotter, and stops the poles from becoming even colder.

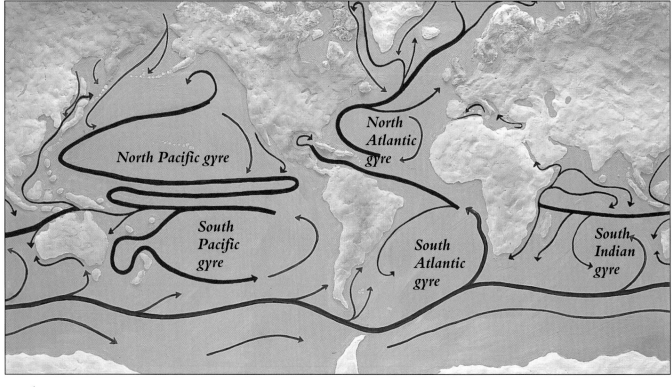

North Pacific gyre

North Atlantic gyre

South Pacific gyre

South Atlantic gyre

South Indian gyre

🌊 Deep-ocean currents

Currents in the deep ocean were discovered only recently. They move more slowly than surface currents—less than 350 feet (105 m) a day. Deep-ocean currents begin in the Arctic and Southern oceans. Cold, extra-salty water sinks to the ocean floor. From the poles, cold water flows along the seabed toward the equator, where it warms up. As cold currents warm up, they become lighter, or less dense, and rise to the surface. Then they flow back to the poles again as warm surface currents.

🌊 Currents and marine life

All living things need oxygen to survive. Ocean currents are very important to marine life because they carry oxygen from the surface to the deep ocean. Water at the ocean surface takes in oxygen from the air. When this water sinks in polar regions, it carries oxygen down with it. Deep-ocean currents traveling along the ocean floor bring oxygen to the creatures that live there. Without ocean currents sinking and rising, there would be no oxygen, and therefore, no life on the ocean floor.

WARM AND COLD CURRENTS TEST

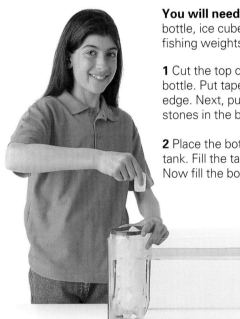

You will need: water, tank, plastic bottle, ice cubes, tape, jug, stones or fishing weights, salt, food coloring

1 Cut the top off an empty plastic bottle. Put tape around the cut edge. Next, put some weights or stones in the bottle.

2 Place the bottle at one end of the tank. Fill the tank with warm water. Now fill the bottle with ice cubes.

3 Fill the jug with ice-cold water, some salt, and food coloring. Gently pour some of the colored water down the outside of the plastic bottle and wait.

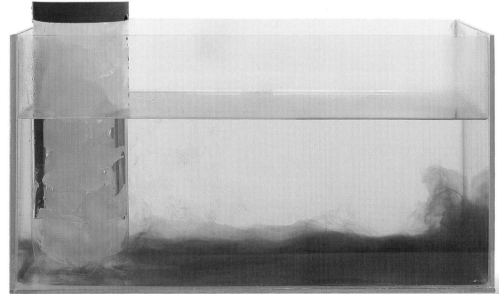

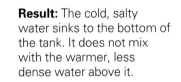

Result: The cold, salty water sinks to the bottom of the tank. It does not mix with the warmer, less dense water above it.

Slowly, the cold water travels to the end of the tank, always staying below the layer of warm water. Eventually, the cold water warms up and mixes with the water above it. It starts to rise, just as cold deep-ocean currents do when they reach warm water at the equator.

17

Waves

Waves can be anything from gentle ripples to huge storm waves crashing against coasts. Since early times, sailors have noticed that when it is windy at sea, the height of the waves is affected. Today we know that wind speed is the most important force in driving ocean waves.

℃ Wind and waves

Most waves are caused by the wind pulling and pushing the surface of the ocean. The size and power of waves depends on the speed of the wind, how long it has been blowing, and how far it has blown. Other types of waves are started by erupting seamounts, earthquakes, and tides.

△ *These surfers are being carried quickly toward the shore by a steep, powerful wave.*

℃ Water in waves

The top of a wave is called the crest, and the bottom is the trough. The distance from one crest to the next is called the wavelength. As waves travel over deep water, they make the water at the surface move in circles. Big waves make water deeper down move in circles too. These circles of moving water get smaller and smaller.

When a wave reaches the shore, the water in the wave starts to move in oval shapes instead of circles. The crest gets higher and steeper, and the distance between waves becomes shorter. The wave slows down, making the crest topple over and break on the shore.

WATCHING WAVE ACTION

You will need: long tank, gravel, tape, paddle

1 Put a layer of gravel on the bottom of the tank. Half fill the tank with water. Mark the water line with tape. Make gentle, steady waves at one end of the tank.

Result: You will see that the distance from the top (crest) of the wave to the water line is the same as the distance from the dip (trough) to the water line.

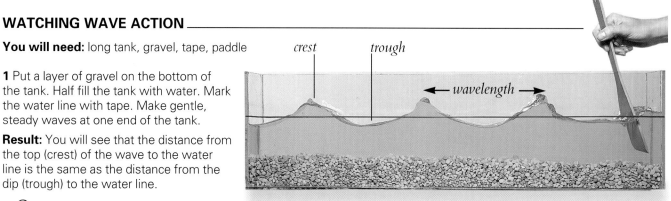

crest   trough   ← *wavelength* →

DEEP WAVE EXPERIMENT

You will need:
long tank, waterproof
glue, 5 pieces of cork,
5 washers, string,
gravel, paddle

1 Cut five different lengths of string. Glue a piece of cork to each end and tie a washer to the other end. Pour gravel into the tank. Fill the tank with water. Arrange the strings as shown. Make gentle waves near the surface. Only the corks at the top will move. The corks at the bottom stay still because the water is not moving there.

2 Now lower your paddle and make slow, steady waves.

Result: The waves will be bigger than before, and the corks at the bottom of the tank will move. This is because large waves make the water circulate farther down. Strong winds blowing over the ocean make big waves in this way.

ℝ Passing waves

Waves pass through the water. They do not take water with them as they move. You can see this if you watch a bottle on the water. As the waves pass by, the bottle bobs up and down but stays more or less in the same place. The bottle will move slowly over time because it is carried by surface ocean currents.

▽ *The green arrows show how water moves when a wave passes through it.*

ℝ Tsunamis

These destructive waves are caused by erupting seamounts, undersea earthquakes, or by hurricanes, cyclones, or other large storms at sea. Tsunamis typically travel 500 to 600 miles (800 to 970 km) per hour beneath the surface of the open ocean. When the waves reach shallow water, they are forced to slow way down, causing the waves to suddenly rise up and slam down on the land. Such huge waves have caused terrible damage to coasts, killing people and destroying buildings and crops.

water moving in circles *water moving in ovals* *waves closer together near the shore* *crashing wave* *sloping shore*

Tides

Every day, the level of the sea rises and falls. This is called the **tide**. At high tide the sea rises, and at low tide it falls. There are usually two high and two low tides each day. They are caused mainly by the pull of the moon and the sun on the Earth.

☾ The moon's pull
The moon gives off a pulling force, called **gravity**. This force pulls the oceans outward on the side of the Earth nearest the moon. As the Earth spins, these bulges of water move across the ocean like an enormous wave, making the tides rise and fall.

moon

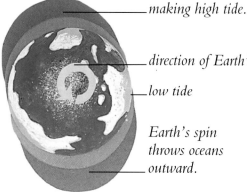

◁ This model shows how the moon's gravity causes tides on Earth.

Oceans are pulled toward the moon, making high tide.

direction of Earth's spin

low tide

Earth's spin throws oceans outward.

☾ Spring and neap tides
The sun also pulls the Earth's oceans, but its pull is weaker because it is much farther away. Twice a month, when the sun, moon, and Earth are in a line, the pull of the sun and the pull of the moon combine. This makes higher and lower tides than usual, called **spring tides**. When the sun, moon, and Earth form a right angle, the sun's pull works against the moon's pull, making less extreme tides called **neap tides**.

▽ These models show how the pull of the moon and sun produce two spring tides and two neap tides each month.

▷ key

effect of moon's gravity on oceans   *effect of sun's gravity on oceans*

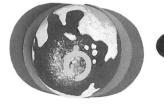

sun

new moon: spring tide
The moon and sun pull together in a straight line.

first quarter: neap tide
The moon and sun pull against each other because they are at right angles.

full moon: spring tide
The moon and sun pull in a straight line.

third quarter: neap tide
The moon and sun are at right angles again and pull against each other.

↻ Tidal range

Along the shore, the difference between **sea levels** at high and low tide is called the tidal range. The average tidal range for an ocean coast is about 10 feet (3 m). Seas that are almost completely surrounded by land, such as the Mediterranean Sea, have smaller tidal ranges.

↻ 🐟 Surviving the tides

Tides affect the marine life that lives on or near the shore. Creatures that can survive out of water for long periods at low tide, live high up the shore. Creatures that need to be in water more of the time, live on the lower shore. When creatures are exposed by low tides, they need to avoid drying out and must hide from predators. Periwinkles, for example, stay in their shells to stay moist. This also protects them from birds.

△ *This is a beach in Scotland at low tide. You can see the tidal zones and some of the plants that live there.*

▽ *This model shows the different areas of the shoreline, called tidal zones, and some of the creatures and plants that live in each zone.*

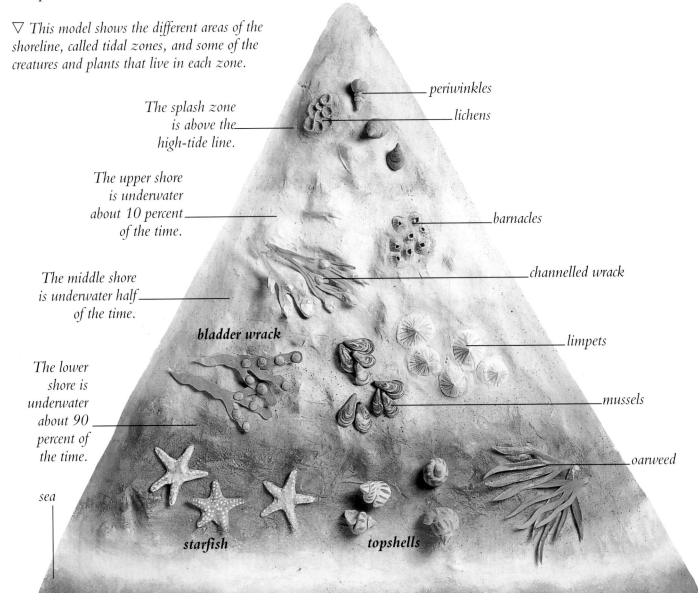

The splash zone is above the high-tide line. — periwinkles — lichens

The upper shore is underwater about 10 percent of the time. — barnacles

The middle shore is underwater half of the time. — channelled wrack

bladder wrack

The lower shore is underwater about 90 percent of the time. — limpets

— mussels

— oarweed

sea

starfish   **topshells**

Changing sea levels

For millions of years, sea levels have risen and fallen. These variations have been caused by changes in climate or by movements deep inside the Earth that alter the shape of the ocean floor. As sea levels change, so do coastlines. Two features that show how sea levels have changed over time are **fjords** and **raised beaches**.

🏔🌡 Rising and falling

As the temperature of the Earth rises and falls, sea levels also rise and fall. During the last 100 years, the Earth has warmed up slightly, and sea levels have risen about 5 inches (12 cm). This is because some of the ice at the poles has melted and because water expands when it is heated. Sea levels also change when forces inside the Earth make the outer crust move up and down, for example, when earthquakes happen.

🏔🌡 Flooded valleys

The last great climate change occurred more than 10,000 years ago when the Earth experienced an **ice age**. At this time, glaciers carved out long valleys in areas such as Norway and Alaska. When the Earth warmed up, some glaciers melted. The level of the sea rose and flooded the valleys, forming long stretches of water called fjords.

▷ *This is a model of a fjord. The valley, formed by a glacier, now lies below the water.*

shallow mouth of valley

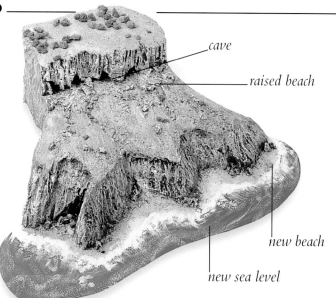

cave

raised beach

new beach

new sea level

△ *This model shows a raised beach. Cliffs and caves that were formed by the sea (see pages 24 and 25) now lie above sea level.*

🏔 Raised beaches

When the land rises, or the sea level falls, old shorelines are sometimes left stranded. These shores form platforms, called raised beaches, which lie above the new level of the sea.

sea level today

valley floor that was once above sea level

👫 Rising sea levels

Today, sea levels are rising, and by the year 2100 they may have risen 15 inches (40 cm). Even such a small rise may cause floods in cities near coasts, such as New York and London. In countries such as Bangladesh, which lies close to sea level, many people could lose their homes and farms to the sea.

▽ *The Thames Barrier was built across the River Thames in England to stop London from being flooded by spring tides and storm waves from the North Sea.*

👫 Sea barriers

As sea levels rise, more people are having to build barriers to protect themselves and their cities from high tides and storm waves. In 1953, almost 2,000 people in the Netherlands and 300 people in Britain were killed when huge waves from the North Sea swept across low areas of land.

In the Netherlands, permanent sea walls have been built to prevent another disaster. In London, a mechanical barrier lies across the River Thames. It is raised during spring tides when there is a danger of flooding and when there are storm waves.

This side of the barrier lies toward the sea.

Steel gates are raised to hold back a spring tide.

When ships need to pass, the gates can be lowered so that they lie below the level of the riverbed.

Arms on these piers raise the gates back up from the riverbed.

Coasts

The place where ocean meets land is called the coast. Coastlines are always changing shape. Wind and waves wear away some coasts and build up others. Coasts that are being worn away by waves are called eroding coasts. Powerful waves eat into the land, forming steep cliffs and deep caves.

Hard and soft rocks

The shape of an eroding coast depends partly on the type of rock the land is made of. Soft rocks, such as limestone, wear away more easily than hard rocks, such as granite. Headlands are rocky outcrops jutting out from the coast. They are usually made of hard rock. Bays, which are carved into the coast, are made of softer rocks.

▽ *This model shows some features of an eroded coast.*

Pebble and water power

The main way in which the sea wears away the land is by hurling sand and pebbles against it. This makes pieces of the land break off. The force of the waves crashing against rocks also helps break rocks into smaller pieces.

Air power

As waves pound against the coast, they force air into cracks in the rocks. When the waves pull back, the forced air spreads out quickly and explodes out of the cracks, weakening the rock.

Changing coastlines

When waves approach a shallow shore, they slow down gradually and travel along the coast. But when a wave meets a headland in deep water, it still has a great deal of energy, or power. This power erodes headlands more quickly than sheltered bays. Over time, waves will wear away a headland, leaving a straight coastline.

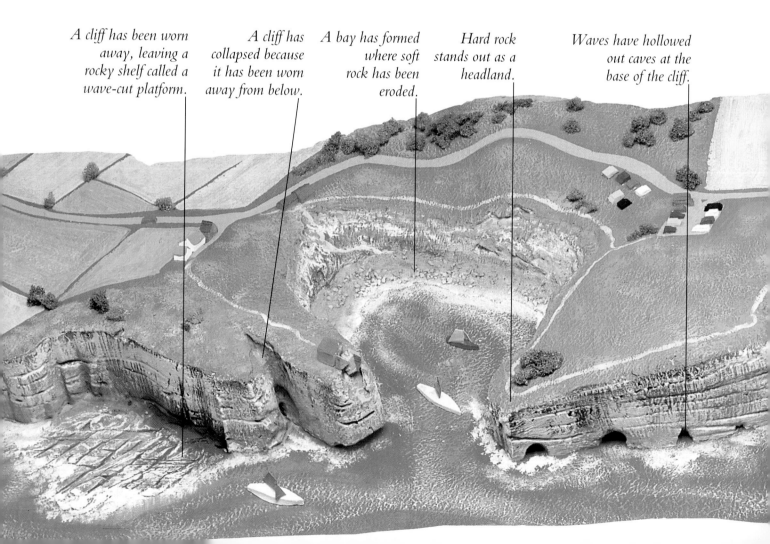

A cliff has been worn away, leaving a rocky shelf called a wave-cut platform.

A cliff has collapsed because it has been worn away from below.

A bay has formed where soft rock has been eroded.

Hard rock stands out as a headland.

Waves have hollowed out caves at the base of the cliff.

🪨 ℛ How caves form

When the sea crashes against rocky cliffs, cracks appear in natural joints in the rock. Eventually, due to constant wave erosion, the cracks become bigger and bigger until a large hole, or cave appears. Waves constantly pushing and compressing the air in a cave may punch a hole through the roof of the cave. This is called a blowhole.

🪨 ℛ Arches and stacks

In some places, two caves form on opposite sides of a headland. If they grow large enough, they may meet in the middle to form an arch. The sea continues to widen the arch until the roof, or lintel, falls, leaving behind a pillar of rock called a stack.

△ *Living at the edge of an eroding coast can be dangerous. As a coast becomes unstable, large sections may fall into the sea in landslides.*

An arch forms where two caves on either side of a headland meet.

A hole in the roof of a cave is called a blowhole.

A headland has been worn away, leaving a series of stacks.

A lighthouse warns ships that rocks from collapsed cliffs lie underwater close to shore.

Coasts

🏔 📜 New land from waves

When coasts are eroded, the sea carries away loose rocky material, such as sand and pebbles. Some of this sediment is swept out to sea, but some is carried along the coast and deposited in sheltered bays. Over time, the deposited sediment forms new land, such as a beach. Sand and mud are also carried into the sea by rivers. This sediment settles around the mouths of rivers to form mud flats and salt marshes.

📜 🏔 Longshore drift and spits

In some places, waves hit the coast at an angle. They travel across the beach and then fall down in a straight line. The waves follow a zigzag path, dragging sediment with them along the coast. The sideways movement of waves is called longshore drift. Where this happens, sea walls called groynes are built along the beach to stop longshore drift. When a coastline curves or changes direction, longshore drift may wash sand and pebbles out to sea, forming a ridge called a spit. Spits often curve because waves push them back toward the coast.

▽ *This model shows some of the features of a growing coast, where waves drop sediment to build up new land.*

△ *Salt marshes make good feeding and breeding grounds for birds. This salt marsh is on the Atchafalaya Delta in Louisiana. It is fed by the waters of the Gulf of Mexico.*

🏔 Tombolos and lagoons

When a spit forms between an island and the coast, linking the two, it makes a tombolo. In other places, spits extend from one headland to another and seal off bays from the sea, creating **lagoons**. Over a long period of time, plants start to grow in the lagoon and eventually it turns into dry land.

Two headlands are joined by a spit, creating a lagoon.

Waves have pushed the tip of this spit into a hook shape.

Fine sediment has been deposited in a bay, forming a beach.

🏖 Bars and barrier islands

Bars are ridges of sediment that build up parallel to gently sloping shores. Unlike spits, bars are not joined to the coast, and they are made of material from the seabed, not the coast. If a bar breaks the sea surface, plants grow and the bar becomes a barrier island. Miami Beach, Florida, is an example of a barrier island.

🏖 Mudflats and salt marshes

Behind spits and bars, or at the mouth of a river, seawater is shallow and protected from waves. Over time, mud and sand drop out of the water and create mud flats. Plants that can survive in salt water grow on the mud. The plants help form a more solid structure called a salt marsh.

🏖 Sand dunes

Sand dunes may form behind salt marshes or mud flats. The wind blows loose sand inland and it piles up into small hills called dunes. Plants such as certain grasses grow on the dunes. Their spreading roots help bind the sand and stop it from being blown away.

LONGSHORE DRIFT EXPERIMENT

You will need:
large tray, water, sand, paddle, 3 long pieces of wood

1 Make a narrow beach along one side of the tray. Pour water in the other side of the tray.

2 Paddle from one corner of the tray toward the sand.

Result: All the sand will drift across the tray. This is what happens when waves break at an angle along beaches.

3 Arrange the sand as before and wedge the wood in the sand as shown. Paddle again.

Result: This time, the wood stops the sand from drifting across the tray, just as groynes do on a beach.

A tombolo is a spit that joins an island to the coast.

Groynes stop waves from carrying sediment along the coast.

Wind blows loose sand into dunes.

Mud flats form at the mouth of a river.

Plants grow on a mudflat, making a salt marsh.

Coral reefs

Coasts are also shaped by tiny marine animals called polyps. They live in warm, shallow waters and create brilliantly colored structures called coral reefs. Polyps are soft creatures with hard outer cases called coral. When polyps die, they leave the coral behind. Over time, millions of corals build up to form walls called reefs. A coral reef may start off as a fringing reef. As it grows, it may become a barrier reef, and later, an atoll.

△ *This is part of the Great Barrier Reef. Polyps only live at the top of the reef. The rest of the coral is dead.*

▶ 🐠 Fringing and barrier reefs

A fringing reef is a flat reef of living coral joined to a coast, like the reefs around the Hawaiian Islands. Barrier reefs are long, coral ridges separated from the coast by lagoons. The Great Barrier Reef, off the coast of Australia, stretches for about 1,250 miles (2,010 km) and is the largest structure ever made by living creatures. It is so big that astronauts could see it from the moon.

▶ 🐠 Atolls

An atoll is a ring- or horseshoe-shaped wall of coral built up from a sunken bank or crater with a shallow lagoon in the middle. As soil lodges on the reef, plants grow there, and the reef becomes a coral island. The Maldive and Seychelle islands are atolls in the Indian Ocean.

How coral atolls form

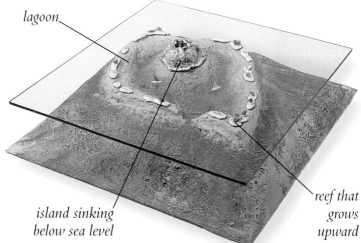

island formed by underwater volcano

fringing reef around island's coast

lagoon

island sinking below sea level

reef that grows upward

1 Fringing reef

When seamounts, or underwater volcanoes, erupt above sea level, they form volcanic islands. Polyps are attracted to the warm, mineral-rich waters around the shores of these islands. Over time, a small wall of coral forms at the edge of the coast.

2 Barrier reef

After hundreds or thousands of years, the island may sink, or the sea level may rise. The coral wall continues to grow upward because polyps need light to survive. The coral forms a barrier reef, creating a lagoon between the reef and the island.

MAKE A VOLCANIC ISLAND

You will need: plastic bottle, tubing, scissors, baking soda, chicken wire, newspaper strips, flour-and-water paste, paint, jug, vinegar, red food coloring, large square board

1 Cut the bottle in half. Carefully cut three holes so that the tubes fit in securely.

2 Fill the bottle up to the first tube with baking soda. Place the bottle on the board. Make a volcano shape around it with the wire. Cover with newspaper strips dipped in the paste.

3 Make sure the ends of the tubes poke through the frame. Leave a large hole in the top, above the bottle. Let your volcano dry, then paint it.

4 Pour some vinegar into a jug—about the same amount as the baking soda. Add red food coloring.

5 Slowly pour the vinegar into the hole at the top and stand back!

Result: The volcano erupts and lava (the soda) pours out. In real life, the lava cools and becomes a volcanic island. In warm waters, coral reefs will grow around the island.

An atoll forms when an island sinks below the sea.

Deep water lies on the seaward side of the atoll.

3 Atoll

When an island disappears below the surface of the sea, a deep ring of coral, called an atoll, is left behind. The lagoon in the middle is shallow, but the seaward side of the atoll is surrounded by deep water.

A shallow lagoon is formed in the middle of the atoll.

29

Black smokers

One of the most exciting discoveries in oceanography happened in 1977. Scientists found hot water gushing up through cracks in the ocean floor called **deep-sea vents**. The water contains dissolved minerals. When the hot water cools, the minerals become solids and form tall chimneys. Colored water escapes from the chimneys, so these vents are often called black smokers or white smokers.

△ *Deep-sea vents in the Pacific Ocean are rich in giant crabs and other marine life.*

Birth of a deep-sea vent

Vents occur along the mid-ocean ridges. Seawater seeps down through cracks in the crust toward the hot rocks below. As the rocks heat the water to extreme temperatures, water dissolves minerals out of the surrounding rocks. The hot water then shoots back up through the crust. Cold seawater from above cools the hot water. The dissolved minerals harden and form chimneys.

Pacific and Atlantic vents

The first vents to be discovered were in the eastern Pacific, off the coast of South America. Oceanographers think that these sites may be between 100 and 1,000 years old. Vent communities have also been discovered along the Mid-Atlantic Ridge. These sites are thought to be much older, and have been smoking for tens of thousands of years.

MAKE A BLACK SMOKER

You will need: tall tank, water, gravel, fish-tank thermometer, small plastic bottle, small fishing weights, food coloring, two lengths of narrow tubing, modeling clay, wooden skewer, waterproof tape

1 Fill the tank with cold water. Tape the thermometer to the inside of the tank. Put gravel on the bottom.

2 Put some weights into the bottle to make it heavy. With an adult's help, fill the bottle with very hot water and food coloring.

3 Feed both tubes into the bottle so that they reach the bottom. Mold the clay around the tubes to seal the top of the bottle. Plug one tube with the skewer.

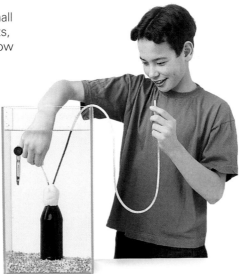

4 Record the temperature, then place your bottle (chimney) and the plugged tube into the tank. Remove the skewer and blow gently through the other tube until a layer of hot, colored water sits on top of the cold water. Record the temperature again.

Result: The hot, colored water will make the temperature in the tank rise slightly. Real black smokers make the temperature of surrounding waters very hot.

❧ Pacific vents

In the Pacific, many large and unusual animals, such as giant tubeworms, giant crabs, and clams, live in the warm water that surrounds deep-sea vents. About 95 percent of these animals have never been seen anywhere else on Earth. Unlike other animals in the ocean or on land, most vent creatures do not eat plants or other animals (see page 32). Instead, they feed on microbes that feed off the minerals which pour out of the vents.

❧ New discoveries

Deep-sea vents have only recently been discovered, so there are still many mysteries waiting to be solved. For instance, how many deep-sea vents are there in all the world's oceans? Why do vent creatures grow so big, and how quickly do they do this? Do creatures travel from vent to vent, and if so, how?

▽ *This model shows a submersible investigating the creatures living around vents in the Pacific Ocean.*

Each of the Russian Mir submersibles have been used to study vents.

Smoke rises several hundred feet above the seabed.

Chimneys are, on average, 50 to 65 feet (15 to 20 m) tall.

Giant tubeworms grow up to 12 feet (3.7 m) long.

Giant white clams are the size of a dinner plate.

Marine life

All ocean life can be divided into three groups: plankton, animals that swim freely in the sea, and creatures that live on or near the ocean floor. Plant life is only found near the surface, where there is sunlight, but animals are found at all depths.

▷ *This model shows some of the creatures that live in the world's oceans.*

▽ *Key to the model.*

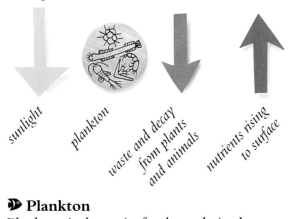

sunlight   plankton   waste and decay from plants and animals   nutrients rising to surface

❱ Plankton
Plankton is the main food supply in the oceans. There are two types of plankton: plantlike organisms called phytoplankton, and animals called zooplankton. Like plants on land, phytoplankton need light to make food and survive. They are eaten by zooplankton and some larger animals. Zooplankton include tiny baby fish and shrimplike krill. They swim for some food but mostly are carried by ocean currents.

❱ Food chains
In the ocean, as on land, most creatures either eat plants or other animals. Each plant or animal is like a link in a chain. A series of five or six animals feeding on each other is called a **food chain**. Animals from one food chain may feed on animals in other food chains. If there is a change in one link in a food chain, then this may affect creatures in the other chains.

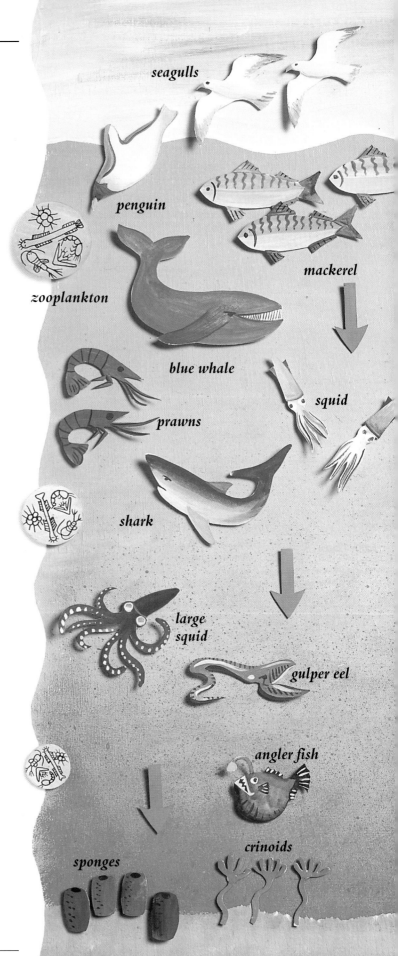

seagulls

penguin

zooplankton

mackerel

blue whale

squid

prawns

shark

large squid

gulper eel

angler fish

crinoids

sponges

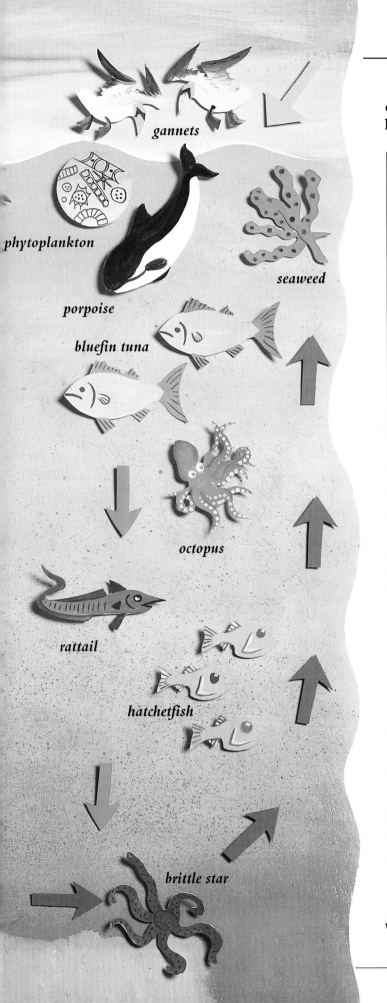

gannets

phytoplankton

porpoise

seaweed

bluefin tuna

octopus

rattail

hatchetfish

brittle star

What lives in the oceans?

ocean levels

sea level

upper waters

600 ft. (180 m)

midwaters

3,000 ft. (900 m)

deep sea

⚷ 🐟 Upper waters

The upper waters of the ocean receives the most light and heat. Phytoplankton and all ocean plants live here. Many animals also live in this zone because they need the warm temperatures to survive and because there is a large food supply.

🐟 Midwaters

Below the upper waters, the sea is cold and dark, and there are no plants. Animals feed on each other or on animal and plant remains that float down from above. Many fish, such as the hatchetfish, glow in the dark to attract prey or to find mates.

🐟 Deep sea

In the darkness of the ocean deep, many fish are blind. They feel their way around the seabed. Some deep sea animals, such as sponges, are fixed to the seabed. Others crawl or burrow in the sediment. Animals feed on each other or on remains falling from above. In the cold temperatures, fish such as the angler fish grow slowly and live much longer than those on the surface. Since food is more scarce, fish, such as the gulper eel, have huge mouths and stretchy stomachs so they can eat as much as possible when they find a meal.

℃ 🐟 Upwelling

In some areas, winds cause surface waters near the coast to move offshore, allowing colder, deeper waters rich in minerals and dissolved plant and animal remains to rise to the surface. This is called **upwelling**. The nutrients carried by the upwelling provide food for marine life near the surface, which is an important reason why these areas have great numbers of fish.

Deep-sea sediments

A constant rain of particles falls, like snow, onto the ocean floor. These particles come from soil and rocks on land, from erupting seamounts, from the remains of sea creatures, and even from space. The particles have built up layers of sediment that are millions of years old. By studying sediments, scientists can find out what happened on Earth in the past.

⛰ Turbidity currents

Rivers wash enormous amounts of sediment onto the continental shelf. Every few thousand years, this sediment may be dislodged, perhaps by an earthquake or other disturbance. Then sediment flows quickly across the shelf and down the continental slope. Currents of moving sediment are called **turbidity currents**. They have the power to cut huge valleys, called submarine canyons, in the continental slope. When a turbidity current reaches the abyssal plain, it fans out and slows down.

▽ *This model shows how a turbidity current carries material from the edge of a continent to the deep sea. This may happen over just a few weeks.*

A river on land washes sediment onto the continental shelf.

A turbidity current creates a submarine canyon.

This continental slope plunges to depths of 2¼ miles (3.6 km).

A turbidity current carries sediment onto the abyssal plain.

continental shelf

abyssal plain

🏔 From sediments to rock

In the deep ocean, sediments washed off the land mix with other kinds of sediments, such as plant remains, animal skeletons, and bits of shell and coral. As layers of sediment build up, particles are pressed together, and the water is squeezed out. Over millions of years, soft sediments are turned into hard sedimentary rocks.

🏔 👥 Deep-sea cores

Most sediments in the deep ocean build up over a long time. It takes 1,000 years to lay down one-third inch (1 cm) of sediment. Oceanographers use special drills to dig into the seabed and take samples, called deep-sea cores, of sedimentary rocks. These cores tell us about climate changes and ocean currents millions of years ago.

Oceanographers also study the sediments in cores to find out how the Earth has changed over time. Sediments show that about 20,000 years ago, the Earth was experiencing an ice age. Gradually, the Earth warmed up and as this happened, the type of sediments deposited on the ocean floor changed.

▷ *This is a model of a deep-sea core 31 inches (80 cm) deep. The sediments were laid down between 7,000 and 20,000 years ago.*

▽ *Key to the sediments on the model*

volcanic dust and ash

dust carried in air

shells and coral

sea plants

rocks and soil

sand from land

bony animal remains

7,000 years ago

All the sediment in this part of the core was dropped by a turbidity current. It was laid down in just a few weeks, 7,000 years ago.

Larger, heavier pieces of sediment, such as sand and gravel, sank to the bottom of the turbidity current.

7,000 years ago

This layer of sediment took 6,000 years to form.

13,000 years ago

This layer formed over 7,000 years, during an ice age.

20,000 years ago

Ocean resources

The world's oceans contain many **resources**. The sea supplies us with food, such as fish and salt, and we make medicine from plankton and coral. We mine beneath the seabed for minerals, such as oil and gas, and make electricity using the power of the tides. We also use sand and gravel sediments in industry.

⚓ 🏭 Where do oil and gas come from?

Oil comes from plants and the bodies of creatures trapped in sedimentary rock millions of years ago. This rock lies deep within the Earth's crust, under the continents and the seabed. Heat and pressure around the rock slowly turn the remains into drops of oil. As this happens, natural gas forms. Most oil and gas is spread through rocks in tiny amounts. But in some places, large amounts collect between layers of very hard rock. At sea, oil rigs drill into the seabed to find these reserves.

▷ *This is an offshore oil-production platform drilling for oil deep beneath the seabed.*

Gas that cannot be used is burned off.

A rig consists chiefly of drilling equipment and a derrick or drilling tower.

The legs of the platform are fixed to the seabed.

Several wells are drilled from one platform to reach as much oil and gas as possible.

Most oil and gas wells are thousands of feet under the sea.

Helicopters bring workers and supplies to and from the platform.

Oil tankers carry tons of oil to land.

Oil is pumped ashore daily.

Layers of rock are laid down over millions of years.

Folds and faults occur in the Earth's crust.

A layer of hard rock forms a lid on top of the oil and gas.

Oil and gas is trapped between layers of hard rock.

Hard rock stops oil and gas from seeping downward.

⚓ 🏔 Other resources

After oil and gas, the most important ocean resources are gravel and sand. These are mined from continental shelves. Many of the world's countries use these sediments for building on land. Salt is another important resource. It accounts for two-thirds of all the minerals in seawater. The oceans contain other minerals, but researchers haven't found an economical way to extract them yet.

⚓ The energy crisis

One problem facing the world is the shortage of energy sources. Oil and gas take millions of years to form. Scientists believe that if we continue to extract the reserves we know about at the current rate, they will be used up in 100 years. We need to find new reserves and new sources of energy to create power.

△ *Most of the world's salt is produced in hot countries, such as Sri Lanka. Shallow pools of seawater are left in the sun. When the water evaporates, salt is left behind.*

⚓ Oil and gas reserves

Most of the known oil and gas deposits on land have already been used up. Oil companies are exploring the oceans more widely in their search for new deposits. In the late 1990's, about two-fifths of the world's oil and gas came from under the oceans. Once oil and gas are pumped to shore, they are refined and used as sources of energy. From oil, we make petroleum, which we use to power cars and engines, to generate electricity, and to make plastics. We use both gas and oil for heating and lighting in homes and in industry.

⚓ ℝ New sources of power

We already know how to produce electricity using the ebb and flow of the tides, but scientists are still trying to find a way to use wave power. They know that when the wind blows over the ocean, energy is transferred to the water, creating waves. If the power of the waves could be harnessed, it would create a never-ending supply of energy.

TEST WAVE ENERGY

You will need: craft knife, 3 plastic bottles, tape, shallow tank, dowel as long as the width of the tank, modeling clay, 2 clothes pins, water, large paddle

1 Ask an adult to help you cut the top off the bottles and cut the bottles in half lengthwise. Make a hole in the end of each bottle half as shown.

2 Slide the two halves of each bottle into each other and tape as shown. Thread all the bottles, or floats, onto the dowel. They should swing freely.

3 Attach the ends of the dowel to the tank with clay. The floats should not touch the bottom of the tank. Support the dowel with clothes pins . Now, fill the tank halfway with water.

4 Move the paddle toward the floats.

Result: The barrier will swing gently, and water will ripple more on one side of it than the other because the floats take up some of the energy of the water. If used on a large scale at sea, this energy could be used to turn an engine, which could then produce electricity.

Ports and settlement

For thousands of years, people have lived by the sea so that they can fish and earn a living. Today, 60 percent of the world's population lives on or near the coast. Many people live in large cities that have grown up around ports used for fishing or trading. Ports are places where ships can load and unload close to sailable waters. Most of the world's trade is carried out from large ports, such as New York, Rotterdam, and Yokohama.

△ *This is a small coastal village in Vietnam. Most of the people who live here earn their living through fishing.*

♙♙ ☙ Fishing for a living

Nowadays, most fishing is done from large fishing ports by a relatively small number of people who use ships called trawlers. Modern trawlers have huge nets and electronic equipment to help locate the catch. Modern trawlers catch millions of tons of fish every year. However, most of the world's fishermen live in small coastal towns and villages. They catch far fewer fish because they use simple hooks and lines, or baskets and nets.

▽ *These cities are also the world's busiest ports. They handle most of the ocean-going trade around the world.*

♙♙ World ports

Most of the world's trade is handled by large ports at the edges of the oceans. Ports are often at points where rivers meet the sea because goods can be easily transported inland by river to other towns. Rotterdam, in the Netherlands, is near the mouth of the river Rhine and is the world's busiest port. Other ports are in natural bays along coasts, where ships can shelter from the open sea. The port of San Francisco is in the world's largest natural bay.

Arkhangel'sk
Vancouver
Rotterdam
Yokohama
San Francisco
New York
New Orleans
Hong Kong
Port Said
Mumbai
Dakar
Singapore
Lima
Lobito
Mombasa
Sydney
Rio de Janeiro
Freemantle
Buenos Aires
Capetown

♟ An ideal port

San Francisco port is one of the busiest ports in the world. It was developed in the 1850's on the western shores of San Francisco Bay. It is an ideal place for a port for several reasons. Firstly, the bay is wide and deep, so it can take many ships. The bay is also on the shores of the Pacific Ocean, which makes it ideally placed for trade with South America, Hawaii, Australia, Japan, and other parts of Asia. Lastly, when the port was first established, ships heading north to hunt whales needed a clear route to the Arctic Ocean. San Francisco provided a convenient place to start from or to stop off.

▷ *You can see on this map how San Francisco Bay is sheltered from the Pacific Ocean.*

Golden Gate Bridge crosses the entrance to the bay.

This red area is the city of San Francisco.

Oakland Bridge

The port of San Francisco grew on the east side of the city.

◁ *This model shows the main port area of San Francisco today.*

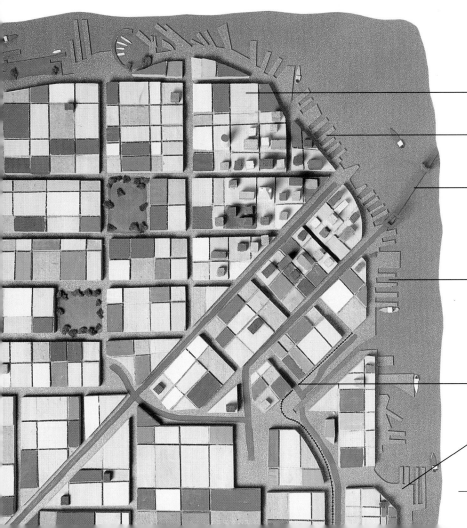

This area is the oldest part of the port and the city.

Some of the shore once lay under the sea, but it was drained to extend the port.

Oakland Bridge leads to the newer port of Oakland.

Huge ocean-going carriers, such as container ships and RoRo (Roll-on/Roll-off) cargo ships, load and unload all along these piers.

Goods arriving at the port are carried by rail to the rest of the United States.

Grain and steel are stored in large terminals before being shipped abroad.

Exploring oceans

Oceans have always been difficult places to explore because of the lack of air, the bitter cold, and the extreme pressure. The first pieces of equipment invented to help divers stay underwater were diving bells, but they did not hold much air. Today, submersibles are built to withstand pressure and supply enough oxygen for oceanographers to explore the ocean floor for up to eight hours.

▽ *This is a model of **Alvin** investigating giant tubeworms near a deep-sea vent.*

👥 Breathing underwater

In the past, the biggest problem exploring the ocean floor was how to breathe underwater. In 1690, Edmund Halley invented the diving bell. A large wooden bell was lowered to the seabed by rope from a ship at the surface. Air trapped inside the bell and in barrels close by, supplied divers on the ocean floor. It wasn't until 250 years later, in the 1940's, that two Frenchmen, Jacques Cousteau and Emile Gagnan, invented equipment that allowed divers to carry their own air. This invention was called **scuba**.

Pressure in the cabin is the same as at sea level.

still camera

video camera

spotlights

Side thrusters push Alvin *backward and forward.*

The porthole allows the crew to view the deep-ocean floor.

The basket holds samples of rocks and sediment.

DIVING BELL EXPERIMENT

You will need: clear plastic bottle, craft knife, plastic tubing, modeling clay, tall tank, water, gravel

1 Ask an adult to cut the bottom off the bottle. Feed the tube into the bottle. Seal the top with clay. Then cover the bottom edge with clay. Place gravel in the tank and fill with water.

2 Cover your end of the tube so that no air escapes. Hold the bell upright and push it down so that it touches the gravel. The water level may rise a little inside the bell, but the air in the bell will stop it from filling up.

3 Modern diving bells have an air supply to drive the water out of the bell. To remove the water from your bell, blow into the tube. If it were a full-size diving bell, divers could now work on the seabed, on the area covered by the bell.

♦♦ Submersibles

People cannot dive below about 165 feet (50 m) because of the immense pressure in the ocean. **Submersibles**, such as *Alvin*, carry people down to depths of a maximum of 14,764 feet (4,500 m), although the *Mir* submersibles can go down farther. Using these special underwater craft, oceanographers observe the deep sea and deep-seabed close-up.

A mechanical arm collects samples of rocks, seawater, and tubeworms.

♦♦ Undersea robots

Undersea robots are called ROV's, which stands for Remote Operated Vehicles. These are sent down to collect information when conditions are too dangerous for divers. ROV's are attached by cables to a research ship or submersible so that they can be controlled automatically from a distance. ROV's take photographs and collect rock and sediment samples from the ocean floor. They can also stay underwater much longer than people—for months at a time if necessary.

♦♦ Taking measurements

Satellites in space are also used to explore the oceans. They take measurements of the ocean surface. They record the temperature of the ocean surface and provide important information about ocean currents and sea ice. To monitor the oceans depths, oceanographers place other instruments in the seawater. Such instruments include cameras, echo-sounders for mapping the ocean floor (see pages 42 and 43), and machines that measure water density, temperature, and depth.

Mapping the seabed

In the past, the only way of finding out the depth of the ocean was to lower a weighted rope from the side of a ship and measure the rope. Now, sound waves beamed underwater are used to build "sound pictures" of the seabed. Satellites in space can also tell us about the shape of the seabed.

👥✎ Mapping with sound

Since the 1920's, the invention of sonar has made it much easier to map the seabed. A ship sails in a line, towing a device that sends pulses of sound straight down into the water. Oceanographers time how long it takes for the sound echoes to bounce back from the seabed. They know how far sound travels in a certain time, so they can work out the distance to the seabed. Using the same method, people on research ships beam signals to fixed points on land to find out where they are.

△ Ocean depth was first measured using weighted ropes called plumb lines. Such measurements were used to make the first depth maps.

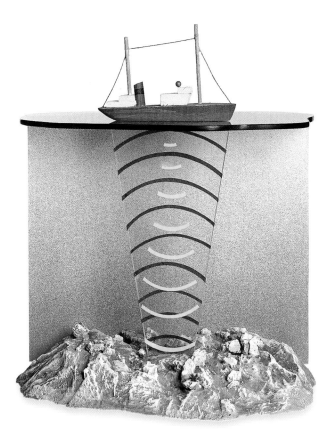

△ Today, sound waves are used to measure depth. The waves are beamed to the seabed (yellow waves), then they bounce back to a research ship (red waves).

👥✎ Using plumb lines

In the 1800's, people first began to understand what the ocean floor might be like. Between 1872 and 1876, a British ship called HMS *Challenger*, took 492 deep-sea measurements around the world using plumb lines. Oceanographers marked each depth measurement on a chart before moving to a new position.

✎ SEASAT

In 1978, the first sea satellite, SEASAT, was launched. For 105 days, it measured the distance between itself and the sea surface. Peaks and valleys on the surface were found to match those on the seabed. For example, the surface of the sea can be dozens of feet higher above mid-ocean ridges or continental shelves than above ocean trenches or abyssal plains.

✎ Faster mapping

A special underwater sonar system called **GLORIA** is towed along the seabed to provide detailed pictures of features such as submarine canyons. It beams two wide fans of sound, building up sound pictures of a much wider area of the bed than ordinary sonar. GLORIA is towed in a straight line up and down sections of an ocean. It is important for a research ship to know exactly where it is, so that it does not map the same area twice. Research ships use satellites in orbit and fixed points on land to determine their position at sea.

A satellite beams information about the ship's position.

A research ship tows GLORIA above the seabed.

A ship uses sonar to determine its position from a fixed point on land.

▷ *This model shows how the seabed is mapped today.*

GLORIA maps a section of the seabed.

area being mapped

Sound waves fan out on either side of GLORIA.

seabed

✎ Making maps

Maps of the seabed are called **bathymetric maps**. They show the depth of the seabed according to information collected by sonar. First, mapmakers plot the depth of the ocean floor as a series of points. Then they join points that are at the same depth, creating a series of lines. Undersea maps are like contour maps of dry land, in which lines join points that are at the same height above sea level.

▷ *This is a map of the seabed in the model above. The deepest parts are dark green, and the shallower areas are pale.*

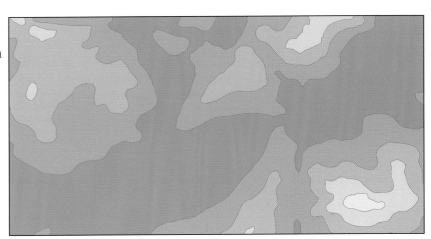

Oceans under threat

People use oceans for trade, travel, tourism, and recreation. We also take food and resources from the oceans. All these activities can have harmful effects on the oceans and the creatures that live in them. Overfishing and pollution are the most common problems. The oceans link all the continents of the world. And because seawater circulates around the globe, what we do in one part of the ocean can affect another.

▷ *This model shows some of the ways that people interact with the oceans and some of the harmful effects they can have.*

⚇ ⥽ Overfishing

In parts of the world, fishing trawlers with huge nets sometimes take too many of the same species of fish from a small area. This means that some ocean waters are overfished. As a result, there are not enough fish left to breed in these areas. This affects other fish in the food chain, and it affects people because there eventually may not be enough fish left to eat. In some places of the world, limits have been set for the number of fish that can be caught at one time.

⚇ ⥽ Threats to marine life

Some species of marine creatures are now rare because too many have been killed for food or sport. Tropical islands and coasts with coral reefs also attract large numbers of tourists every year. Although this helps people develop an understanding of marine life, when corals and shellfish are destroyed by heavy boat anchors and by divers hunting for souvenirs, people are disrupting the natural life cycles of marine life.

Some industries near the coast dump heavy metals directly into the sea.

Much pollution is washed into oceans by rivers.

Coastal cities and ports can damage coastal wildlife.

Offshore drilling collects oil and gas.

Oceanographers monitor the effects of pollution.

Some trawlers overfish.

Submarines patrol the world's oceans.

Two-thirds of the world's cities are on the coast.

Large fishing trawlers can freeze fish on board and stay at sea for months.

Tourists watch whales
migrating to the North Pole.

Oil spilling out of a
supertanker damages
marine life and coasts.

Container ships
carry goods vast
distances across
the ocean.

Sea walls
protect coastal
cities from
high tides
and storm
waves.

Coral reefs and
other marine life are
threatened by
careless tourists.

Small coastal fishing boats
sometimes damage coral reefs.

♀♂ Pollution

One of the biggest threats to the oceans is contamination from industry. Most pollution happens in coastal areas. Heavy industries in coastal cities and ports discharge chemicals and sewage into rivers. The rivers wash the pollutants into the sea. Once they settle on a continental shelf, pollutants form part of the sediment. We do not know a great deal about the long-term effects of pollution. However, we do know that the North and Black seas in Europe have been polluted so much that the marine life is poisoned and may never recover.

△ In 1993, this oil tanker ran aground off the coast of Scotland. It spilled thousands of tons of crude oil, which severely affected local marine life.

♀♂ Possible solutions

All countries of the world need to work together to share ocean resources fairly and to make laws that will prevent overfishing and pollution. It is often difficult to agree on the best way of doing this. It is also hard to make people obey laws when the oceans are so vast and difficult to patrol. The work of oceanographers is vital if we are to understand how best to manage the world's oceans now and in the future.

Glossary

abyssal plain The vast, flat ocean floor beyond the continental slope and continental rise. It is covered with a thick layer of sediment.

Alvin A submersible able to work at depths up to 14,764 feet (4,500 m) and for up to eight hours. Alvin was the first submersible used to explore deep-sea vents in the Pacific.

bathymetric map A map showing ocean depth and ocean peaks and valleys.

continental shelf The gently sloping shelf along the edges of continents. It ends in a steep slope called the continental slope. Sediments dropped at the bottom of the continental slope form the continental rise.

coral reef A structure built in warm waters from the hard remains of small animals called polyps, or corals. There are three kinds of reefs: fringing reefs, barrier reefs, and atolls.

Coriolis effect The way that the spin of the Earth makes the winds and ocean currents bend. They bend to the right north of the equator and to the left south of the equator.

deep-sea vent A crack in the seabed through which hot water and minerals erupt. Vents are usually found along mid-ocean ridges. They are sometimes called black or white smokers.

Earth's plates The Earth's outer crust is broken into about 30 moving pieces called plates. The continents and oceans sit on top of these plates.

fjord A narrow, steep-sided inlet of ocean. It is formed when the ocean floods into a coastal valley that has been dug out by a glacier.

food chain A group of living things arranged in the order in which they feed on each other.

geology Studying the Earth's history by looking at the rocks that make up the Earth's crust.

glacier A large "river" of moving ice on land. Glaciers are formed when layers of snow are compressed together.

GLORIA A type of sonar device that is towed underwater. It is used to make maps of large areas of ocean floor.

gravity An invisible force that pulls things down to the ground and gives them weight.

guyot An underwater seamount with a flat top.

gyre A vast circle of moving water. There are five main gyres in the world's oceans, all of which are made up of the paths of ocean currents.

ice age A period of time in the Earth's history when glaciers and ice sheets covered large parts of the land. The last ice age ended about 10,000 years ago.

lagoon A shallow stretch of seawater partly or completely separated from the open ocean by a narrow strip of land, such as a reef or a spit.

magma Hot liquid rock below the Earth's surface. Sometimes magma rises up through the Earth's crust. When the hot rock cools, it forms new land or new ocean floor.

mantle This is a layer of hot, flowing rocks that lies between the Earth's crust and the core.

mid-ocean ridge A long, narrow chain of underwater mountains that has formed where two of the Earth's plates moved apart and magma spilled out onto the ocean floor.

neap tide The tide with the smallest difference between high and low tide. This tide happens when the sun, Earth, and moon are at a right angle.

ocean basin A great depression in the Earth's crust that is filled with ocean or sea. An ocean basin does not include the continental shelf.

ocean current A "river" of water flowing in the oceans. There are two main types of currents: surface currents, which carry warm water from the equator to the poles; and deep-water currents which carry cold water from the poles to the equator.

ocean trench A long, narrow valley under the sea, usually near a continental shelf, where old ocean floor is being pushed down inside the Earth.

oceanographer A person who studies the science of the oceans.

plankton Plankton are a vital link in ocean food chains. There are two main types: tiny plantlike organisms called phytoplankton; and animal, or zooplankton, which can swim, but not well.

raised beach A rocky platform above a beach. It forms when the sea level falls or the land rises.

resources A stock or supply of something that can be used if necessary. The oceans are full of natural resources, such as food and minerals.

satellite An unmanned spacecraft placed in orbit around the Earth. The first satellite to be launched for oceanographic research was SEASAT. Satellites are vital for mapping the surface of the oceans.

scuba This stands for self-contained underwater breathing apparatus. A diver carries a tank of air that is kept at the same pressure as sea level, so that the diver can breathe underwater.

sea level The average level of the sea around the world.

seamount A large underwater volcano. If a seamount grows enough to rise above the ocean surface, it forms a volcanic island.

sediment Loose particles of rocks or living things that stick together to form mud, sand, or silt. Sediment settles on the continental shelf or the ocean floor. When loose sediments are pressed tightly together over millions of years, they form sedimentary rock.

sonar An instrument that uses sound echoes to measure distances and locate objects.

spring tide The tide with the greatest difference between high and low tide. It happens when the sun, Earth, and moon are all in a line.

submersible A vehicle that can withstand the pressure and cold water in the deep ocean.

tide The rise and fall of the oceans each day. It is caused by the gravity of the moon and the sun and the spin of the Earth.

turbidity current A huge current of sediment flowing down a continental slope. It usually occurs close to where a river flows onto the continental shelf.

upwelling The process by which winds move warm surface waters offshore, allowing cold, nutrient-rich waters to rise up from the ocean floor to the surface.

Index